The noise underneath my bed

Written and designed by
Umesh Chhetry

©2020 Umesh Chhetry

It was already two hours past Sophie's bedtime, but Sophie couldn't sleep. She was worried about her first day at a new school.
Suddenly she heard a noise in-between the slats of her wooden bed , a strange, sound echoed around her room.

What was hiding under her bed?

Sophie took a deep breath and had a look, but there was nothing there. Sophie thought she must have just imagined it, but every time she closed her eyes she could hear the noise **coming from under her bed.**

The next morning, Sophie didn't feel like eating her breakfast. "*Are you ok, dear?*" her mother asked. Worried about starting at a new school and the noises she had heard under her bed, she put on a brave face and replied, **"I'm okay."**

While at school, Sophie couldn't concentrate.
She kept thinking about what might be beneath her bed.
Could it be a monster? Or maybe a ghost?
Could it be just her imagination?

As she sat at her desk, Sophie's teacher announced "We have a new student joining us today" **Sophie felt shy.** "So that we can get to know you better Sophie…" her teacher continued.

'...why don't you do show and tell at the end of the week". Sophie didn't like the idea of speaking in front of the whole class, **just the thought of it made her belly hurt.**

During playtime all the other children ran outside to play but **Sophie was too scared to join in.** So she just waited by herself until it was time to go back inside.

When Sophie got home she went onto her school website and saw so many exciting videos of her follow students. Mia had posted a video of her dancing! Theo was roller skating! And Paula was shown winning a swimming competition! Sophie began to worry: "These girls are so talented; they would never want to be friends with me".

As soon as the **negative thoughts filled her mind,** The noises from under her bed started again! **Sophie was terrified!** She was even more frightened than last time! She couldn't sleep all night trying to block out the **noises.**

By morning , Sophie was exhausted.
"You don't look very well Sophie, maybe we should take you to the doctor?," Sophie's father said.

Sophie didn't want to go to the doctor, she was scared they would give her an injection.
So with a worried look on her face, Sophie simply said *"I'm Okay, no need for the doctor"*.

To Sophie, **nothing was fun anymore.** She didn't find joy in the things that used to make her happy.
She couldn't find a reason to smile. She just felt worried and empty.

After School , Sophie went to her room to have a cry, she worried about the noise's, having no friends, her show and tell. and maybe even an injection at the doctor!

Just then....BONK! BONK! Her bed began to shake uncontrollably as if it was about to break Sophie was terrified...

Finally, Sophie couldn't take it any longer and she ran into her parents' arms and burst into tears. "There's something underneath my bed!"

Her father ran to her room and checked under her bed, but there was **nothing to be found** apart from some old toys.

Sophie's mother gave her a hug, stroked her hair to calm her down, and said: "It seems to me that you have found a Worry Troll". Sophie looked confused but her mother began to explain.

"A **"Worry Troll"** is a bully who is responsible for making us think worrisome thoughts in the back of our minds," she revealed.

"The Worry Troll's job is to keep us from enjoying life. He gets joy from picking on children and adults, making them **feel worried and scared.**"

"You may not be able to see him but you know he is there. but the **more you feed him** with your **worries**...

"How do I get rid of this Worry Troll?" Sophie begged her mother. "It's pretty simple dear," Sophie's mother explained. "You have already taken your first step by letting me know you have a problem."

Sophie's mother then told her to have a look at the computer screen and said. "When ever I hear the Worry Troll I follow these simple rules."

HOW TO DEAL WITH YOUR
WORRY TROLL

Talk to someone

Tell friends and family you're feeling worried, and let them know how they can help you.

Eat well-balanced meal

Do not skip any meals and always eat healthy energy-boosting snacks like fruits.

Exercise daily

Exercising can help you feel good and will make you healthy.

Get enough sleep

When stressed your body needs sleep and rest. it's important to get 8 hours sleep per night.

Do your best

Aiming high is good, but be proud of however close you get.

Take deep breaths

Breath in and out slowly when ever you are feeling stressed.

Why are you worried

Is it social media, school, family or something else? Write in a journal when you're feeling worried and look for a pattern.

Just by reading her mother's list, Sophie could feel **the Worry Troll getting smaller.** That thought comforted her because it meant that she was in control of her mind.

Now whenever Sophie is worried about anything,
she knows she can ask for help.
Over the following weeks, Sophie regained her appetite, presented in front of her class and made lots of friends.

Most importantly, Sophie slept peacefully at night because there were

no more noises coming from underneath her bed.

Signs if your Child has a Worry Troll

Symptoms of a Worry Troll (depression) include:

- Sadness, or a low mood that does not go away
- Being irritable or grumpy all the time
- Not being interested in things they used to enjoy
- Feeling tired and exhausted a lot of the time
- Have trouble sleeping or sleep more than usual
- Not be able to concentrate
- Interact less with friends and family
- Be indecisive
- Not have much confidence
- Eat less than usual or overeat
- Have big changes in weight
- Seem unable to relax or be more lethargic than usual
- Talk about feeling guilty or worthless

If you think Your child has a Worry Troll

If you think your child may be depressed, it's important to talk to them. Try to find out what's troubling them and how they're feeling.

Whatever is causing the problem, take it seriously. It may not seem like a big deal to you, but it could be a major problem for your child.

If your child does not want to talk to you, let them know that you're concerned about them and that you're there if they need you.

Encourage them to talk to someone else they trust, such as another family member, a friend or someone at school.

Any more information please seek professional help.

All information above is taken from the NHS website.

Printed in Great Britain
by Amazon